4.99

Budget Buster

QUICK
& EASY

FEED FOUR OR MORE FOR

$10 OR
LESS!

Love Food ® is an imprint of Parragon Books Ltd

Parragon
Queen Street House
4 Queen Street
Bath BA1 1HE, UK

Copyright © Parragon Book Ltd 2005

Love Food ® and the accompanying heart device is a trademark of Parragon Books Ltd

Internal design by Fiona Roberts
Photography and text by The Bridgewater Book Company Ltd.

ISBN: 978-1-4075-4937-8

Printed in China

NOTE
Cup measurements in this book are for American cups. This book also uses imperial and
metric measurements. Follow the same units of measurement throughout; do not mix
imperial and metric. All spoon measurements are level: teaspoons are assumed to be 5 ml
and tablespoons are assumed to be 15 ml. Unless otherwise stated, milk is assumed to be
whole milk, eggs and individual vegetables such as potatoes are medium, and pepper is
freshly ground black pepper.

The times given for each recipe are an approximate guide only because the preparation times
may differ according to the techniques used by different people and the cooking times may
vary as a result of the type of oven used.

Recipes using raw or very lightly cooked eggs should be avoided by infants, the elderly,
pregnant women, convalescents, and anyone with a chronic condition.

contents

introduction

When it comes to food it sometimes seems that we have to choose between the inexpensive but time-consuming and the costly but convenient. This is not the case—it is possible to prepare and cook delicious and nourishing meals without spending hours slaving over a hot stove or ripping the family budget to shreds. In fact, it's astonishingly easy and all it really needs is a slight adjustment in the way you think about cooking quickly—and the recipes in this book, all of which can be prepared from scratch and cooked in under an hour.

We tend to believe that only expensive cuts of meat, such as steak and pork tenderloin, can be cooked quickly and to some extent this is true, but if you shift your perspective slightly, you will discover that it's not invariably the case. Meatballs and stir-fries, for example, are among the speediest, easiest, and most economical dishes to prepare and taste just great. Chicken is always good value for money and it's a well-kept secret that the cheaper, dark meat has much more flavor than the more expensive breast portions. In any case, it makes budgetary sense to buy a whole chicken and cut it into pieces yourself than to buy already prepared portions.

Nutritionists advise us to eat five portions of fruit and vegetables a day and because they cost much less than meat and poultry, the bank manager would probably agree. In every sense it is worth considering the occasional vegetarian option, especially if you bear in mind that seasonal vegetables are usually much less expensive than non-seasonal, imported ones. Moreover, most vegetables taste better and retain more nutrients when they are cooked quickly. Also, don't overlook those natural "convenience" foods like eggs and cheese. They can form the basis of numerous delicious dishes, can be made in moments and cost little more than a few cents.

BUDGETING GUIDE	
$	Bargain
$$	Budget
$$$	Economical

Shopping

Plan your menus in advance, write a shopping list, and stick to it. Try to avoid dashing around the supermarket in your lunch hour, grabbing the first thing you see or, even more expensive, stocking up on ready-meals. Frozen and chilled dishes are rarely as good as the pictures on the packaging, often fail to satisfy the appetite, and never taste as delicious as home cooking. Ready-made sauces don't really save very much time, are usually packed with added flavorings, colorings, and preservatives, and cost a silly amount of money

compared with, say, a can of tomatoes, a few herbs, and an onion, or a little flour, butter, milk, and grated cheese. You can rustle up a much tastier tomato or cheese sauce at home in no time at all for a fraction of the cost.

There are lots of quick dishes to make using the simplest of ingredients

Time and Money

■ Scissors are often quicker to use than a knife when chopping some ingredients, such as herbs and bacon.

■ Many people have kitchen equipment that they hardly every use. If you have a food processor or blender, take advantage of its time-saving qualities for chopping, slicing, shredding, grating, and making bread crumbs (don't throw away stale bread—crumb it instead).

Delicious meals can be created in minutes, even on a budget!

■ It's quicker, easier, and less wasteful to peel vegetables such as parsnips and potatoes after cooking and they retain more nutrients too.

■ When baking potatoes, push a metal skewer through the centers. This speeds up the cooking time and therefore lowers energy costs.

■ When buying chicken, always choose fresh. If you buy a frozen bird, you may be paying for as much as ten percent water.

■ In the case of meat products, such as sausages, cheapest is rarely the best value. Quite apart from the disappointing flavor, they tend to burst during cooking unless you cook them very gently and slowly. They often leak large amounts of fat so you end up with a rather unappetizing end product.

tomato sauce

- makes about 14 oz
- prepared in 5 minutes
- cooks in 4 - 6 minutes

1 tbsp vegetable oil
2 garlic cloves, crushed
14 oz canned chopped tomatoes
dash of Tabasco sauce
salt and pepper

1 Heat the oil in a skillet and cook the garlic, stirring frequently, for 2-3 minutes. Add the tomatoes and their can juice and bring to the boil, stirring. Boil over high heat, stirring and scraping up the sediment from the base of the skillet, for 2-3 minutes until thickened.

2 Remove the skillet from the heat, season to taste with salt and pepper, and stir in the Tabasco.

soups, snacks & sides

Most people know that homemade soup is an economical

dish, but you may be surprised to learn that you don't have to cook

it for hours and it still tastes wonderful. So too, do the other

dishes in this chapter, whether you serve them as appetizers,

light meals, or accompaniments.

\$\$

broccoli soup

■ serves 6

■ prepared in 10 mins

■ cooks in 20 - 25 mins

12 oz/350 g broccoli

1 leek, sliced

1 celery stalk, sliced

1 garlic clove, crushed

12 oz/350 g potato, diced

4 cups vegetable stock

1 bay leaf

freshly ground black pepper

crusty bread or toasted

   croutons, to serve

1 Cut the broccoli into florets and set aside. Cut the thicker broccoli stalks into $1/2$-inch/1-cm dice and put into a large pan with the leek, celery, garlic, potato, stock, and bay leaf. Bring to a boil, then reduce the heat, cover, and let simmer for 15 minutes.

2 Add the broccoli florets to the soup and return to a boil. Reduce the heat, cover, and let simmer for an additional 3–5 minutes, or until the potato and broccoli stalks are tender.

3 Remove from the heat and let the soup cool slightly. Remove and discard the bay leaf. Purée the soup, in small batches, in a food processor or blender until smooth.

4 Return the soup to the pan and heat through thoroughly. Season to taste with pepper. Ladle the soup into warmed bowls and serve at once with crusty bread or toasted croutons.

1   1   1

carrot soup

$$

- serves 6
- prepared in 10 mins
- cooks in 20 mins

2 oz/55 g butter
2 onions, grated
salt and pepper
1 lb 9 oz/700 g carrots, grated
1 large potato, grated
2 tbsp grated orange rind

6–7 cups boiling water
juice of 1 large orange
2 tbsp chopped fresh parsley,
  to garnish

1 Melt the butter in a large, heavy-bottom pan. Add the onions and cook over medium heat, stirring constantly, for 3 minutes. Sprinkle with a little salt, add the carrots and potato, then cover, reduce the heat, and cook for 5 minutes.

2 Stir the orange rind into the pan, then add enough boiling water to cover. Return to a boil, cover, and let simmer briskly for 10 minutes. Add the orange juice.

3 Remove the pan from the heat and let cool slightly, then pour into a food processor and process until a smooth purée forms. Alternatively, use a hand-held electric blender to purée the soup in the pan. Return the soup to the pan, adding a little more boiling water if it is too thick. Return to a boil, taste and adjust the seasoning if necessary, and ladle into warmed soup bowls. Garnish with chopped parsley and serve immediately.

tomato & bell pepper soup

$$

- serves 4
- prepared in 15 mins
- cooks in 35 mins

2 large red bell peppers
1 large onion, chopped
2 stalks celery, trimmed and
   chopped
1 garlic clove, crushed
2½ cups vegetable bouillon
2 bay leaves
4 cups canned plum tomatoes
salt and pepper
2 scallions, finely shredded,
   to garnish
crusty bread, to serve

1 Preheat the broiler to hot. Halve and seed the peppers, arrange them on the broiler rack, and cook, turning occasionally, for 8–10 minutes until soft and charred.

2 Let the bell peppers cool slightly, then carefully peel off the charred skin. Reserving a small piece for the garnish, chop the bell pepper flesh and place it in a large pan.

3 Mix in the onion, celery, and garlic. Add the bouillon and the bay leaves. Bring to a boil,

cover, and simmer for 15 minutes. Remove from the heat.

4 Stir in the tomatoes and transfer to a blender. Process for a few seconds until the mixture is smooth, then return it to the pan.

5 Season the soup with salt and pepper to taste and heat for 3–4 minutes until piping hot. Ladle into warm bowls and garnish with the reserved bell pepper, cut into strips, and the shredded scallion. Serve with crusty bread.

1

2

4

chicken noodle soup

$$$

- serves 4-6
- prepared in 10 mins
- cooks in 25 mins

1 sheet of dried egg noodles
from a 9 oz/250 g pack

1 tbsp oil

4 skinless, boneless chicken
thighs, diced

1 bunch scallions, sliced

2 garlic cloves, chopped

2 tsp finely chopped fresh
gingerroot

3½ cups chicken bouillon

scant 1 cup coconut milk

3 tsp red curry paste

3 tbsp peanut butter

2 tbsp light soy sauce

1 small red bell pepper,
chopped

½ cup frozen peas

salt and pepper

1 Put the noodles in a shallow dish and soak in boiling water as instructed on the package.

2 Heat the oil in a large preheated pan or wok.

3 Add the diced chicken to the pan or wok and cook for 5 minutes, stirring until lightly browned.

4 Add the white part of the scallions, garlic, and ginger, and cook for 2 minutes, stirring.

5 Stir in the chicken bouillon, coconut milk, red curry paste, peanut butter, and soy sauce.

6 Season with salt and pepper to taste. Bring to a boil, stirring, then simmer for 8 minutes, stirring occasionally.

7 Add the red bell pepper, peas, and green scallion tops and cook for 2 minutes.

8 Add the drained noodles and heat through. Spoon the chicken noodle soup into warmed bowls and serve with a spoon and fork.

1

3

8

tomato soup with spinach & chickpeas

$$

- serves 4
- prepared in 5 mins
- cooks in 15 mins

2 tbsp olive oil
2 leeks, sliced
2 zucchini, diced
2 garlic cloves, crushed
4 cup canned chopped
  tomatoes

1 tbsp tomato paste
1 fresh bay leaf
3½ cups vegetable bouillon
14 oz/400 g can garbanzo
  beans (chickpeas), drained
  and rinsed

8 oz/225 g spinach
freshly-grated Parmesan
  cheese, to serve

1 Heat the oil in a large pan, then add the leeks and zucchini and cook them briskly for 5 minutes, stirring constantly.

2 Add the garlic, tomatoes, tomato paste, bay leaf, vegetable bouillon, and garbanzo beans.

1

3 Bring the soup to a boil and simmer for 5 minutes.

4 Shred the spinach finely, add to the soup, and cook for 2 minutes. Season to taste.

2

5 Discard the bay leaf. Serve the soup immediately with freshly grated Parmesan cheese and warm sun-dried tomato bread.

NOTE: If you invest in a block of fresh Parmesan it can be stored in the refrigerator for a long period and thus becomes an economical ingredient.

4

hearty bean soup

■ serves 6
■ prepared in 15 mins
■ cooks in 20 mins

10½ oz/300 g canned cannellini
beans, drained and rinsed
10½ oz/300 g canned cranberry
beans, drained and rinsed
about 2½ cups chicken or
vegetable stock
4 oz/115 g dried conchigliette or
other small pasta shapes
4–5 tbsp olive oil
2 garlic cloves, very finely
chopped
3 tbsp chopped fresh flat-leaf
parsley
salt and pepper

1 Place half the cannellini and half the cranberry beans in a food processor with half the chicken stock and process until smooth. Pour into a large heavy-bottom pan and add the remaining beans. Stir in enough of the remaining stock to achieve the consistency you like, then bring to a boil.

2 Add the pasta and return to a boil, then reduce the heat and cook for 15 minutes, or until just tender.

3 Meanwhile, heat 3 tablespoons of the oil in a small skillet. Add the garlic and cook, stirring constantly, for 2–3 minutes, or until golden. Stir the garlic into the soup with the parsley. Season to taste with salt and pepper and ladle into warmed soup bowls. Drizzle with the remaining olive oil to taste and serve immediately.

1   2   3

pasta & lentil soup

$$

- serves 4
- prepared in 5 mins
- cooks in 25 mins

4 strips bacon, cut into small
  squares
1 onion, chopped
2 garlic cloves, crushed
2 celery stalks, chopped
1¾ oz/50 g farfalline or
  spaghetti, broken into
  small pieces

14 oz/400 g canned brown
  lentils, drained
5 cups hot vegetable stock
2 tbsp chopped fresh mint
fresh mint sprigs, to garnish

1   Place the bacon in a large skillet together with the onion, garlic, and celery. Dry fry for 4–5 minutes, stirring, until the onion is tender and the bacon is just beginning to brown.

2   Add the pasta to the skillet and cook, stirring, for 1 minute to coat the pasta in the fat.

3   Add the lentils and the stock, and bring to a boil. Reduce the heat and let simmer for 12–15 minutes, or until the pasta is tender but still firm to the bite.

4   Remove the skillet from the heat and stir in the chopped fresh mint. Transfer the soup to warmed soup bowls, garnish with fresh mint sprigs, and serve immediately.

$

zucchini pancakes

- makes 16 - 30
- prepared in 5 - 10 mins
- cooks in 20 mins

3½ oz/100 g self–rising flour

2 eggs, beaten

2 fl oz/50 ml milk

10½ oz/300 g zucchini

2 tbsp fresh thyme

1 tbsp oil

salt and pepper

1 Sift the self-rising flour into a large bowl and make a well in the center. Add the eggs to the well, and using a wooden spoon, gradually draw in the flour.

2 Slowly add the milk to the mixture, stirring constantly to form a thick batter.

3 Meanwhile, wash the zucchini. Grate the zucchini over a sheet of kitchen paper placed in a bowl to absorb some of the juices.

4 Add the zucchini, thyme and salt and pepper to taste to the batter and mix thoroughly.

5 Heat the oil in a large, heavy-based skillet. Taking a tablespoon of the batter for a medium-sized pancake or half a tablespoon of batter for a smaller-sized pancake, spoon the mixture into the hot oil and cook, in batches, for 3–4 minutes on each side.

6 Remove the pancakes with a perforated spoon and drain thoroughly on absorbent kitchen paper. Keep each batch of pancakes warm in the oven while making the rest. Transfer to serving plates and serve hot.

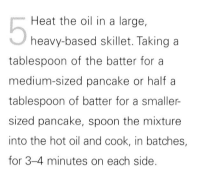

1   3   4

bean burgers

- serves 4
- prepared in 15 mins
- cooks in 20 mins

1 tbsp sunflower oil, plus
  extra for brushing
1 onion, finely chopped
1 garlic clove, finely chopped
1 tsp ground coriander
1 tsp ground cumin

5 oz/115 g white
  mushrooms,
  finely chopped
1½ cups canned red pinto or
  red kidney beans, drained
  and rinsed

2 tbsp chopped fresh
  flat-leaf parsley
all-purpose flour, for dusting
salt and ground black pepper
burger buns and salad,
  to serve

1 Heat the oil in a heavy skillet. Add the onion and cook, stirring occasionally, for 5 minutes, until soft. Add the garlic, coriander, and cumin and cook, stirring frequently, for 1 minute more. Add the mushrooms and continue to cook, stirring constantly, for 4–5 minutes until all the liquid has evaporated. Transfer the mixture to a bowl.

2 Place the beans in a small bowl and mash with a potato masher or fork. Stir the beans into the mushroom mixture with the parsley and season to taste with salt and pepper.

3 Dust with flour. Divide the mixture into 4 portions and shape each into a flat, round patty. Brush with oil and cook under a preheated broiler for 4–5 minutes on each side. Serve immediately in burger buns with salad.

2

3

broiled potatoes with lime mayo

$$

- serves 4
- prepared in 10 mins
- cooks in 15 - 20 mins

1 lb/450 g potatoes,
  unpeeled and scrubbed
3 tbsp butter, melted
2 tbsp chopped fresh thyme
paprika, for dusting

LIME MAYONNAISE
2/3 cup mayonnaise
2 tsp lime juice
finely grated zest of 1 lime
1 garlic clove, crushed
pinch of paprika
salt and pepper

1 Cut the potatoes into 1/2 inch/1 cm thick slices.

2 Cook the potatoes in a pan of boiling water for 5–7 minutes—they should still be quite firm. Remove the potatoes with a perforated spoon and drain thoroughly.

3 Line a broiler pan with aluminum foil, and place the potato slices on the foil.

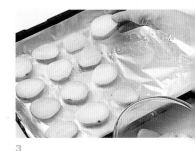
3

4 Brush the potatoes with the melted butter and sprinkle the chopped thyme on top. Season to taste with salt and pepper.

5 Cook the potatoes under a preheated medium broiler for 10 minutes, turning them over once.

4

6 Meanwhile, combine the mayonnaise, lime juice, lime zest, garlic, paprika, and salt and pepper to taste, in a bowl.

7 Dust the hot potato slices with a little paprika and serve immediately with the lime mayonnaise.

6

tomato rice

■ serves 4

■ prepared in 15 mins

■ cooks in 15 - 20 mins

6 tomatoes

1 tbsp oil

1 large onion, finely chopped

1 tbsp curry paste

1 tsp ground coriander

1 tsp ground cumin

salt and pepper

scant 1 cup basmati rice

2½ cups chicken or vegetable stock

2 tbsp chopped fresh cilantro

8 pappadams, to serve

1 Cut 4 of the tomatoes in half and cut out the cores, then set aside. Coarsely chop the remaining tomatoes and set aside until required.

2 Heat the oil in a large pan. Add the onion and cook until softened. Add the reserved tomato halves, curry paste, ground coriander, cumin, and salt and pepper to taste and cook for 2–3 minutes.

3 Add the rice and stir-fry for 2–3 minutes. Add the stock and let simmer for 10–12 minutes, or until the rice is tender and the tomatoes have pulped into the mixture. Remove the tomato skins where possible.

4 Mix the reserved chopped tomatoes and cilantro together in a bowl and stir into the rice mixture. Serve at once with pappadams.

2   3

quick potato with mushrooms

- serves 4
- prepared in 10 mins
- cooks in 35 mins

1½ lb/675 g cubed potatoes
1 tbsp olive oil
2 garlic cloves, crushed
1 green bell pepper, cubed
1 yellow bell pepper, cubed
3 tomatoes, diced
3 oz/85 g white mushrooms,
  halved

1 tbsp vegetarian Worcester
  sauce
2 tbsp chopped basil
salt and pepper
fresh basil sprigs, to garnish
warm crusty bread, to serve

1 Cook the potatoes in a pan of boiling salted water for 7–8 minutes. Drain well and reserve.

2 Heat the olive oil in a large, heavy skillet and cook the potatoes for 8–10 minutes, stirring until browned.

3 Add the garlic and bell peppers to the skillet and cook for 2–3 minutes.

4 Stir the tomatoes and mushrooms into the mixture and continue to cook, stirring, for a further 5–6 minutes.

5 Stir in the Worcester sauce and basil and season well.

6 Transfer to a warmed serving dish, garnish with the fresh basil, and serve at once with crusty bread.

tuna & bean salad

$

- serves 4
- prepared in 30 mins
- cooks in 0 mins

**1 small white onion or
  2 scallions, finely chopped
2 x 14 oz cans butter beans,
  drained
2 medium tomatoes
6½ oz can tuna, drained
2 tbsp flat-leaf parsley, chopped
2 tbsp olive oil
1 tbsp lemon juice
2 tsp clear honey
1 garlic clove, minced**

1 Place the chopped onions or scallions and butter beans in a bowl and mix well to combine.

2 Using a sharp knife, cut the tomatoes into wedges.

3 Add the tomatoes to the onion and bean mixture.

4 Flake the tuna with a fork and add it to the onion and bean mixture together with the parsley.

5 In a screw-top jar, mix together the olive oil, lemon juice, honey, and garlic. Shake the jar until the dressing emulsifies and thickens.

6 Pour the dressing over the bean salad. Toss the ingredients together using 2 spoons and serve.

1   2   5

egg fried rice

- serves 4
- prepared in 20 mins
- cooks in 10 mins

¾ cup long-grain rice

3 eggs, beaten

2 tbsp vegetable oil

2 garlic cloves, crushed

4 scallions, chopped

1 cup cooked peas

1 tbsp light soy sauce

pinch of salt

shredded scallion, to garnish

1 Cook the rice in a pan of boiling water for 10–12 minutes, until almost cooked, but not soft. Drain well, rinse under cold water and drain again.

2 Place the beaten eggs in a pan and cook over a gentle heat, stirring until softly scrambled.

3 Heat the vegetable oil in a preheated wok or large skillet, swirling the oil around the bottom of the wok until it is really hot.

4 Add the crushed garlic, scallions, and peas and sauté, stirring occasionally, for 1–2 minutes. Stir the rice into the wok, mixing to combine.

5 Add the eggs, light soy sauce, and a pinch of salt to the wok or skillet and stir to mix the egg in thoroughly.

6 Transfer the egg fried rice to serving dishes and serve garnished with the shredded scallion.

chow mein

$

- serves 4
- prepared in 5 mins
- cooks in 20 mins

9½ oz/275 g egg noodles

salt

3–4 tbsp vegetable oil

1 small onion, finely
   shredded

scant 1 cup fresh bean
   sprouts

1 scallion, finely shredded

2 tbsp light soy sauce

few drops of sesame oil

1 Cook the egg noodles in a wok or pan of salted boiling water for 4–5 minutes, or according to the package directions.

2 Drain the noodles well and rinse in cold water, then drain thoroughly again. Transfer to a large bowl and toss with a little vegetable oil.

3 Heat the remaining vegetable oil in a preheated wok or large skillet until really hot.

1

4 Add the shredded onion to the wok and stir-fry for 30–40 seconds.

5 Add the bean sprouts and drained noodles to the wok, then stir and toss for an additional 1 minute.

2

6 Add the shredded scallion and light soy sauce and blend well.

7 Transfer the noodles to a warmed serving dish, then sprinkle with the sesame oil and serve immediately.

5

$$$

chicken fritters

- makes 8
- prepared in 10 mins
- cooks in 20 mins

2½ cups mashed potatoes, with
   butter added
1 cup cooked chicken, chopped
½ cup finely chopped cooked ham
1 tbsp dried mixed herbs
2 eggs, lightly beaten
salt and pepper
milk
2 cups fresh brown bread crumbs
corn oil, for shallow-frying
fresh parsley sprigs, to garnish
mixed salad, to serve

1 Blend the mashed potatoes, chicken, ham, herbs, and 1 beaten egg together in a large bowl. Season well with salt and pepper.

2 Shape the mixture into flat patties or small balls. Add a little milk to the second beaten egg.

3 Place the bread crumbs on a plate. Dip the patties in the egg and milk mixture, then roll in the bread crumbs to coat them completely.

4 Heat the oil in a large skillet and cook the fritters until they are golden brown. Garnish with a fresh parsley sprig and serve with a mixed salad.

1

2

3

main meals

This chapter features lots of one-pot dishes, which save both time

and the cost of fuel as the whole meal is cooked at once. Others

need only rice, pasta, or potatoes, which can cook simultaneously,

to accompany them. Whichever you choose, there is a recipe to suit

all tastes from hot and spicy to mellow and melt-in-your-mouth.

baked chicken with french fries

$$

- serves 4
- prepared in 10 mins
- cooks in 35 mins

4 small baking potatoes
1 tbsp sunflower oil
2 tsp coarse sea salt
2 tbsp all-purpose flour
pinch of cayenne pepper
½ tsp paprika pepper
½ tsp dried thyme

8 chicken drumsticks, skin
  removed
1 egg, beaten
2 tbsp cold water
1 cup dry white bread crumbs
salt and pepper
coleslaw to serve

2

1 Preheat the oven to 400°F/200°C. Wash and scrub the potatoes and cut each into 8 equal portions. Place in a clean plastic bag and add the oil. Seal and shake well to coat.

2 Arrange the fries, skin side down, on a non-stick cookie sheet. Sprinkle over the sea salt and bake in the oven for 30–35 minutes until they are tender and golden.

3

3 Meanwhile, mix the flour, spices, thyme, and seasoning together on a plate. Press the chicken drumsticks into the seasoned flour to lightly coat.

4 On one plate mix together the egg and water. On another plate sprinkle the bread crumbs. Dip the chicken drumsticks first in the egg and then in the bread crumbs. Place on a non-stick cookie sheet.

4

5 Bake the chicken drumsticks alongside the fries for 30 minutes, turning after 15 minutes, until both potatoes and chicken are tender and cooked through.

6 Drain the fries thoroughly on paper towels to remove any excess fat. Serve with the chicken, accompanied with lowfat coleslaw and corn relish.

$$

barbecued chicken

- serves 4
- prepared in 5 mins
- cooks in 20 mins

12 chicken drumsticks
SPICED BUTTER
6 oz/175 g/¾ cup butter
2 garlic cloves, crushed
1 tsp grated ginger root
2 tsp ground turmeric
4 tsp cayenne pepper

2 tbsp lime juice
3 tbsp mango chutney
crisp green seasonal salad
**   and boiled rice, to serve**

1 To make the Spiced Butter mixture, beat the butter with the garlic, ginger, turmeric, cayenne pepper, lime juice, and chutney until well blended.

2 Using a sharp knife, slash each chicken leg to the bone 3-4 times.

3 Cook the drumsticks over moderate hot coals for about 12-15 minutes or until almost cooked. Alternatively, broil the chicken for about 10-12 minutes until almost cooked, turning halfway through.

4 Spread the chicken legs liberally with the butter mixture and continue to cook for a further 5-6 minutes, turning and basting frequently with the butter until golden and crisp. Serve the chicken legs hot or cold with a crisp green salad and rice.

1

2

3

chicken & corn skewers

$$

- serves 6
- prepared in 10 mins
- cooks in 20 mins

3 corn cobs

12 chicken wings

1 inch/2.5 cm piece of fresh
  gingerroot

6 tbsp lemon juice

4 tsp sunflower oil

1 tbsp golden superfine sugar

jacket potatoes

1 Remove the husks and silks from the corn. Using a sharp knife, cut each cob into 6 slices.

2 Place the corn in a large bowl with the chicken wings.

3 Peel and grate the ginger root or chop very finely. Place in a bowl and add the lemon juice, sunflower oil, and golden superfine sugar. Mix together until thoroughly combined.

4 Toss the corn and chicken in the ginger mixture to coat evenly.

5 Thread the corn and chicken wings alternately onto metal or pre-soaked wooden skewers to make turning easier.

6 Cook under a preheated moderately hot broiler or on a barbecue grill for about 15–20 minutes, basting with the gingery glaze and turning frequently until the corn is golden brown and tender and the chicken is cooked. Serve immediately with baked potatoes or salad.

1

3

5

chicken stir-fry

$$$

- serves 4
- prepared in 10 mins
- cooks in 15 mins

⅔ cup hot chicken stock

2 tbsp creamed coconut

1 tbsp corn oil

8 skinless, boneless chicken
thighs, cut into long, thin strips

1 small fresh red chili, thinly
sliced

4 scallions, thinly sliced

4 tbsp smooth or crunchy
peanut butter

finely grated rind and juice of 1
lime

freshly cooked rice, to serve

scallion tassels and fresh red
chilies, to garnish

1 Place the stock in a measuring jug and crumble the creamed coconut into the stock, stirring to dissolve.

2 Heat the oil in a large, heavy-bottom skillet or a preheated wok. Add the chicken strips and cook, stirring, until golden.

3 Add the sliced red chili and the scallions to the skillet and cook gently for a few minutes, stirring to mix all the ingredients.

4 Add the peanut butter, coconut mixture, and lime rind and juice, and simmer uncovered, stirring, for 5 minutes. Serve with rice, garnished with a scallion tassel and a red chili.

1   3   4

mexican chicken

$$

- serves 4
- prepared in 5 mins
- cooks in 35 mins

2 tbsp oil
8 chicken drumsticks
1 medium onion, finely chopped
1 tsp chili powder
1 tsp ground coriander
14 oz can chopped tomatoes

2 tbsp tomato paste
⅔ cup frozen corn
salt and pepper
rice and mixed bell pepper salad,
   to serve

1 Heat the oil in a large skillet, add the chicken drumsticks and cook over a medium heat until lightly browned. Remove the chicken drumsticks from the pan with a draining spoon and set aside until required.

2 Add the chopped onion to the pan and cook for 3–4 minutes until softened, then stir in the chili powder and coriander and cook for a few seconds, stirring briskly so the spices do not burn on the bottom of the pan. Add the chopped tomatoes with their juice and the tomato paste and stir well to incorporate.

3 Return the chicken drumsticks to the pan and simmer the casserole gently for 20 minutes until the chicken is tender and thoroughly cooked. Add the corn and cook for a further 3–4 minutes. Season with salt and pepper to taste.

4 Serve with rice and mixed bell pepper salad.

chicken with peppers

$$

- serves 4
- prepared in 5 mins
- cooks in 25 mins

10 skinless, boneless chicken
   thighs
1 medium onion
1 each medium red, green,
   and yellow bell peppers
1 tbsp sunflower oil
14 oz can chopped tomatoes
2 tbsp chopped fresh parsley
pepper
whole wheat bread and a green
   salad, to serve

1 Using a sharp knife, cut
the chicken thighs into bite-
sized pieces.

2 Peel and thinly slice the
onion. Halve and seed the
bell peppers and cut into small
diamond shapes.

3 Heat the oil in a shallow
skillet. Add the chicken
and onion and sauté quickly
until golden.

4 Add the bell peppers, cook
for 2–3 minutes, stir in the
tomatoes and parsley, and
season with pepper.

5 Cover tightly and simmer for
about 15 minutes, until the
chicken and vegetables are
tender. Serve hot with whole
wheat bread and a green salad.

1   2   4

chili con carne

$$

- serves 4
- prepared in 15 mins
- cooks in 45 mins

3 tbsp vegetable oil

1 lb/450 g ground beef

1 onion, chopped finely

1 green bell pepper, deseeded and diced

2 garlic cloves, chopped very finely

1 lb 12 oz/800 g canned chopped tomatoes

14 oz/400 g canned red kidney beans, drained and rinsed

1 tsp ground cumin

1 tsp salt

1 tsp sugar

1–3 tsp chili powder

2 tbsp chopped fresh cilantro

1

1 Prepare the ingredients. Heat the oil in a large flameproof casserole over medium–high heat. Add the beef and cook, stirring, until lightly browned.

1

2 Reduce the heat to medium. Add the onion, bell pepper, and garlic. Cook for 5 minutes, or until soft.

3 Stir in the remaining ingredients. Bring to a boil. Simmer over medium–low heat, stirring frequently, for 30 minutes.

1

4 Stir in the cilantro just before serving.

$$

beef & mushroom casserole

- serves 4
- prepared in 15 mins
- cooks in 35 mins

3 tbsp olive oil
14 oz/400 g ground beef
1 onion, chopped finely
1 bell pepper, deseeded and chopped finely
2¼ cups sliced mushrooms
2 tbsp tomato paste
1¼ cups long grain rice
2½ cups hot beef stock
salt and pepper
scant ¾ cup freshly grated Cheddar

1 Prepare the ingredients. Heat the oil in a high-sided, lidded casserole over medium–high heat. Add the beef and cook, stirring, until lightly browned.

2 Reduce the heat to medium. Add the onion, bell pepper, mushrooms, and tomato paste. Cook for 5 minutes, or until soft.

3 Stir in the rice. Cook gently, stirring, for 3–4 minutes.

4 Pour in the hot stock. Season with salt and pepper. Bring to a boil. Cover tightly and simmer over low heat for about 20 minutes, or until the rice is tender and has absorbed most of the liquid.

5 Sprinkle with the cheese. Cover and let stand while the cheese melts. Serve immediately, straight from the dish.

1   1   1

sausage with lentils

- serves 4
- prepared in 10 mins
- cooks in 25 mins

1 tbsp corn oil
8 oz/225 g spicy sausages,
  sliced
4 oz/115 g rindless smoked
  bacon, chopped
1 onion, chopped
6 tbsp strained tomatoes
generous 1¾ cups beef
  stock

1 lb 5 oz/600 g canned
  lentils, drained and rinsed
½ tsp paprika
2 tsp red wine vinegar
salt and pepper
fresh thyme sprigs,
  to garnish

1 Heat the oil in a large, heavy-bottomed pan. Add the sausages and bacon and cook over medium heat, stirring, for 5 minutes, or until the bacon begins to crisp. Transfer to a plate with a perforated spoon.

2 Add the chopped onion to the pan and cook, stirring occasionally, for 5 minutes, or until softened. Stir in the strained tomatoes and add the stock and lentils. Reduce the heat, cover, and simmer for 10 minutes.

1

3 Return the sausage slices and bacon to the pan, stir in the paprika and red wine vinegar, and season to taste with salt and pepper. Heat the mixture through gently for a few minutes, then serve immediately, garnished with fresh thyme sprigs.

2

3

sausage with onion gravy

$$

- serves 4
- prepared in 5 mins
- cooks in 20 mins

8 pork sausages	**ONION GRAVY**
2 tbsp shortening or	2 tbsp corn oil
2 tbsp vegetable oil	1 onion, chopped
3 eggs	1 tbsp all-purpose flour
salt and pepper	scant 1 cup chicken stock
1¼ cups milk	1 tsp red wine vinegar
¾ cup all-purpose flour	salt and pepper

1 Preheat the oven to 450°F/230°C. Using kitchen scissors, cut in between the sausages to separate them, spread them out on a baking sheet and partially cook in the preheated oven for 10 minutes, while you make the batter. Grease the cups of a muffin pan with the shortening, and place in the oven to heat up.

1

2 Using a balloon whisk, lightly beat the eggs with salt and pepper to taste in a small bowl, then add half the milk. Sift the flour into a large bowl, add the egg mixture, and stir until a smooth batter forms. Stir in the remaining milk. Remove the sausages and muffin pan from the oven and place 2 sausages in each cup. Pour in the batter and return to the oven for 10 minutes, or until the batter is puffed up and golden.

3 Meanwhile, make the onion gravy. Heat the oil in a large pan, add the onion and cook over low heat, stirring occasionally, for 5 minutes, or until softened. Sprinkle in the flour and cook, stirring, for 1 minute. Remove the pan from the heat and gradually stir in the chicken stock.

2

4 Return to the heat and bring to a boil, stirring constantly. Stir in the vinegar and season to taste with salt and pepper. Remove the dish from the oven and serve, handing the gravy separately.

3

pork cutlet with tomatoes & olives

$$$

- serves 4
- prepared in 10 mins
- cooks in 25 mins

2 tbsp olive oil

1 large onion, sliced

1 garlic clove, chopped

14 oz/400 g canned tomatoes

2 tsp yeast extract

4 pork cutlets, about
  4½ oz/125 g each

scant ½ cup black olives, pitted

2 tbsp fresh basil, shredded

freshly grated Parmesan
  cheese, to garnish

green vegetables, to serve

1 Preheat the broiler to medium. Heat the oil in a large skillet. Add the onion and garlic and cook, stirring, for 3–4 minutes, or until just starting to soften.

2 Add the tomatoes and yeast extract to the skillet and let simmer for 5 minutes, or until the sauce starts to thicken.

3 Cook the pork cutlets, under the preheated broiler, for 5 minutes on both sides, until the meat is cooked through. Set the pork aside and keep warm.

4 Add the olives and shredded basil to the sauce in the skillet and stir quickly to combine.

5 Transfer the cutlets to warmed serving plates. Top with the sauce, garnish with freshly grated Parmesan cheese, and serve immediately with green vegetables.

1   2   4

pork chops with sage

$$$

■ serves 4

■ prepared in 10 mins

■ cooks in 15 mins

2 tbsp all-purpose flour

1 tbsp chopped fresh sage, or
   1 tsp dried

4 lean boneless pork chops,
   trimmed of excess fat

2 tbsp olive oil

1 tbsp butter

2 red onions, sliced into rings

1 tbsp lemon juice

2 tsp sugar

4 plum tomatoes, quartered

salt and pepper

1

2

3

1 Mix the flour, sage, and salt and pepper to taste on a plate. Lightly dust the pork chops on both sides with the seasoned flour.

2 Heat the oil and butter in a skillet. Add the chops and cook them for 6–7 minutes on each side until cooked through. Drain the chops, reserving the pan juices; keep warm.

3 Toss the onion in the lemon juice and fry along with the sugar and tomatoes for 5 minutes until tender.

4 Serve the pork with the tomato and onion mixture and a green salad.

$$

pork meatballs

- serves 4
- prepared in 10 mins
- cooks in 40 mins

1 lb/450 g ground pork
2 shallots, finely chopped
2 cloves garlic, crushed
1 tsp cumin seeds
½ tsp chili powder
½ cup fresh whole-wheat
  breadcrumbs
1 egg, beaten
2 tbsp sunflower oil

14 oz/400 g canned chopped
  tomatoes, flavoured with
  chili
2 tbsp soy sauce
7 oz/200 g canned water
  chestnuts, drained
3 tbsp chopped fresh cilantro

1 Place the ground pork in a large mixing bowl. Add the shallots, garlic, cumin seeds, chili powder, breadcrumbs, and beaten egg, and mix together well.

2 Form the mixture into balls between the palms of your hands.

3 Heat the oil in a large preheated wok. Add the pork balls and cook, in batches, over a high heat for about 5 minutes or until sealed on all sides.

4 Add the tomatoes, soy sauce, and water chestnuts and bring to a boil. Return the pork balls to the wok, reduce the heat and let simmer for 15 minutes.

5 Scatter with chopped fresh cilantro and serve hot.

lamb with mint

$$$

- serves 4
- prepared in 10 mins
- cooks in 30 mins

2 tbsp corn oil
1 onion, chopped
1 garlic clove, finely chopped
1 tsp grated fresh gingerroot
1 tsp ground cilantro
½ tsp chili powder
¼ tsp ground turmeric
pinch of salt
12 oz/350 g fresh ground lamb

7 oz/200 g canned chopped
  tomatoes
1 tbsp chopped fresh mint
3 oz/85 g fresh or frozen peas
2 carrots, sliced into thin sticks
1 fresh green chili, seeded
  and finely chopped
1 tbsp chopped fresh cilantro
fresh mint sprigs, to garnish

1 Heat the oil in a large, heavy-bottomed skillet or flameproof casserole. Add the onion and cook over low heat, stirring occasionally, for 10 minutes, or until golden.

1

2 Meanwhile, place the garlic, gingerroot, ground cilantro, chili powder, turmeric, and salt in a small bowl and mix well. Add the spice mixture to the skillet and cook, stirring constantly, for 2 minutes. Add the lamb and cook, stirring frequently, for 8–10 minutes, or until it is broken up and browned.

2

3 Add the tomatoes and their juices, the mint, peas, carrots, chili, and fresh cilantro. Cook, stirring constantly, for 3–5 minutes, then serve, garnished with fresh mint sprigs.

3

spaghetti with tuna

$$

- serves 4
- prepared in 10 mins
- cooks in 15 mins

1 lb 2 oz/500 g spaghetti
1 tbsp olive oil
1 oz/25 g/2 tbsp butter
black olives, to serve
SAUCE
7 oz/200 g can tuna, drained
2 oz/60 g can anchovies, drained
9 fl oz/250 ml/1 cup olive oil
9 fl oz/250 ml/1 cup roughly
  chopped fresh, flat-leaf parsley
¼ pint/150 ml/⅔ cup crème
  fraîche
salt and pepper

1 Cook the spaghetti in a large saucepan of salted boiling water, adding the olive oil, for 8–10 minutes or until tender. Drain the spaghetti in a colander and return to the pan. Add the butter, toss thoroughly to coat and keep warm until required.

2 Remove any bones from the tuna and flake into smaller pieces, using 2 forks. Put the tuna in a blender or food processor with the anchovies, olive oil and parsley and process until the sauce is smooth. Pour in the crème fraîche

and process for a few seconds to blend. Taste the sauce and season with salt and pepper.

3 Warm 4 plates. Shake the saucepan of spaghetti over a medium heat for a few minutes or until it is thoroughly warmed through.

4 Pour the sauce over the spaghetti and toss quickly, using 2 forks. Serve immediately with a small dish of black olives, if liked.

2   3   4

tuna casserole

$

- serves 4
- prepared in 5 mins
- cooks in 25 mins

2 tbsp butter, plus
   extra for greasing
scant ¼ cup all-purpose flour
1¼ cups milk
2 oz/55 g Cheddar cheese,
   grated
7 oz/200 g canned tuna in oil

11½ oz/325 g canned corn,
   drained
salt and pepper
2 tomatoes, thinly sliced
2½ oz/70 g plain potato chips

1 Preheat the oven to 350°F/180°C. Melt the butter in a large, heavy-bottom pan. Sprinkle in the flour and cook, stirring constantly, for 1 minute. Remove the pan from the heat and gradually whisk in the milk. Return to the heat, bring to a boil, and cook, whisking constantly, for 2 minutes.

2 Remove the pan from the heat and stir in the grated cheese. Flake the tuna and add it to the mixture with the oil from the can. Stir in the corn and season to taste with salt and pepper.

3 Lightly grease a large ovenproof dish. Line the dish with the tomato slices, then spoon in the tuna mixture. Crumble the potato chips over the top and bake in the preheated oven for 20 minutes. Serve.

$$

tuna rice

- serves 4
- prepared in 10 mins
- cooks in 10 mins

3 tbsp peanut or corn oil

4 scallions, chopped

2 garlic cloves, finely chopped

7 oz/200 g canned tuna in
oil, drained and flaked

6 oz/175 g frozen or canned
corn kernels and bell
peppers

3½ cups cold boiled rice

2 tbsp Thai fish sauce

1 tbsp light soy sauce

salt and pepper

2 tbsp chopped fresh
cilantro, to garnish

1 Heat the peanut oil in a preheated wok or large, heavy-bottomed skillet. Add the scallions and stir-fry for 2 minutes, then add the garlic and stir-fry for an additional 1 minute.

2 Add the tuna and the corn and bell peppers, and stir-fry for 2 minutes.

3 Add the rice, fish sauce, and soy sauce and stir-fry for 2 minutes. Season to taste with salt and pepper and serve immediately, garnished with chopped cilantro.

1

2

3

macaroni & cheese

$

- serves 4
- prepared in 15 mins
- cooks in 20 mins

salt
7 oz/200 g dried elbow
  macaroni
1 onion, sliced
4 hard-cooked eggs, cut into
  fourths
4 cherry tomatoes, halved

3 tbsp dried bread crumbs
2 tbsp finely grated Red
  Leicester cheese
CHEESE SAUCE
3 tbsp butter
5 tbsp all-purpose flour
2½ cups milk

scant 1½ cups grated
  Red Leicester or
  Cheddar cheese
pinch of cayenne pepper

1 Bring a large pan of lightly salted water to a boil. Add the macaroni and sliced onion, return to a boil and cook for 8–10 minutes, or until the pasta is tender, but still firm to the bite (al dente). Drain well and tip the macaroni and onion into an ovenproof dish.

2 To make the cheese sauce, melt the butter in a pan. Stir in the flour and cook, stirring constantly, for 1–2 minutes. Remove the pan from the heat and gradually whisk in the milk. Return the pan to the heat and bring to a boil, whisking constantly. Simmer for 2 minutes, or until the sauce is thick and glossy. Remove the pan from the heat, stir in the cheese, and season to taste with cayenne and salt.

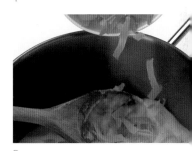

1

3 Pour the sauce over the macaroni, add the eggs, and mix lightly. Arrange the tomato halves on top. Mix the bread crumbs with the finely grated cheese and sprinkle over the surface. Cook under a preheated hot broiler for 3–4 minutes, or until the topping is golden and bubbling. Serve immediately.

2

3

$$

penne with squash *

- serves 4
- prepared in 15 mins
- cooks in 30 mins

2 tbsp olive oil
1 garlic clove, crushed
1 cup fresh white bread crumbs
1 lb 2 oz peeled and seeded
  butternut squash
½ cup water
1 lb 2 oz fresh penne, or other
  pasta shapes
1 tbsp butter
1 onion, sliced
½ cup cooked ham cut into strips
1 cup light cream
½ cup grated Cheddar cheese
2 tbsp chopped fresh parsley
salt and pepper

1 Mix together the oil, garlic, and bread crumbs and spread out on a large plate. Cook on HIGH power for 4–5 minutes, stirring every minute, until crisp and beginning to brown; set aside.

2 Dice the squash. Place in a large bowl with half of the water. Cover and cook on HIGH power for 8–9 minutes, stirring occasionally; leave to stand for 2 minutes.

3 Place the pasta in a large bowl. Add a little salt and pour boiling water to cover by 1 inch over. Cover and cook on HIGH power for 5 minutes, stirring once, until the pasta is just tender, but still firm to the bite. Leave to stand, covered, for 1 minute before draining.

4 Place the butter and onion in a large bowl. Cover and cook on HIGH power for 3 minutes.

5 Coarsely mash the squash, using a fork. Add to the onion with the pasta, ham, cream, cheese, parsley, and remaining water; season generously and mix well. Cover and cook on HIGH power for 4 minutes until heated through.

6 Serve the pasta sprinkled with the crisp garlic crumbs.

2   3   5

* This recipe is cooked in a microwave

garlic spaghetti

$

- serves 4
- prepared in 5 mins
- cooks in 5 mins

½ cup olive oil
3 garlic cloves, crushed
salt and pepper
1 lb/450 g fresh spaghetti
3 tbsp coarsely chopped fresh parsley

1

1 Reserve 1 teaspoon of the oil and heat the remainder in a medium-size pan over low heat. Add the garlic and a pinch of salt, stirring constantly, until golden brown, then remove the pan from the heat. Do not let the garlic burn as it will taint the flavor of the oil. (If it does burn, you will have to start all over again!)

2 Meanwhile, bring a large pan of lightly salted water to a boil. Add the pasta and remaining oil, then return to a boil and cook for 2–3 minutes, or until tender but still firm to the bite. Drain the pasta thoroughly and return to the pan.

3

3 Add the olive oil and garlic mixture to the pasta and toss to coat thoroughly. Season with pepper to taste, then add the chopped parsley and toss well to coat.

4 Transfer the pasta to 4 warmed serving dishes and serve immediately.

3

rice & beans

$$

- serves 4
- prepared in 10 mins
- cooks in 15 mins

6 oz/scant 1 cup long grain rice
4 tbsp olive oil
1 small bell pepper, seeded and
    chopped
1 small bell pepper, seeded and
    chopped
1 onion, finely chopped
1 small red or green chili,
    seeded and finely chopped
2 tomatoes, chopped
4½ oz/½ cup canned red kidney
    beans, rinsed and drained
1 tbsp chopped fresh basil
2 tsp chopped fresh thyme
1 tsp Cajun spice
salt and pepper
fresh basil leaves, to garnish

1 Cook the rice in plenty of boiling, lightly salted water for about 12 minutes, until just tender. Rinse with cold water and drain well.

2 Meanwhile, heat the olive oil in a skillet and fry the green and bell peppers and onion gently for about 5 minutes, until softened.

3 Add the chili and tomatoes, and cook for a further 2 minutes.

4 Add the vegetable mixture and red kidney beans to the rice. Stir well to combine thoroughly.

5 Stir the chopped herbs and Cajun spice into the rice mixture. Season to taste with salt and pepper, and serve, garnished with basil leaves.

2

4

5

spanish tortilla

$

- serves 4
- prepared in 10 mins
- cooks in 35 mins

2 lb 4 oz/1 kg waxy potatoes, thinly sliced
4 tbsp vegetable oil
1 onion, sliced
2 garlic cloves, crushed
1 green bell pepper, deseeded and diced

2 tomatoes, deseeded and chopped
2½ tbsp canned corn, drained
6 large eggs, beaten
2 tbsp chopped fresh parsley
salt and pepper

1 Parboil the potatoes in a pan of lightly salted boiling water for 5 minutes. Drain well.

2 Heat the oil in a large skillet, add the potatoes and onion and then sauté over low heat, stirring constantly, for 5 minutes until the potatoes have browned.

3 Add the garlic, green bell pepper, tomatoes, and corn, mixing well.

4 Pour in the eggs and add the parsley. Season to taste with salt and pepper. Cook for 10–12 minutes until the underside is cooked through.

5 Remove the skillet from the heat and continue to cook the tortilla under a preheated medium broiler for 5–7 minutes or until the tortilla is set and the top is golden brown.

6 Cut the tortilla into wedges or cubes, depending on your preference, and transfer to serving dishes. Serve with salad. In Spain tortillas are served hot, cold or warm.

2

3

4

mushroom stroganoff

$$

- serves 4
- prepared in 5 mins
- cooks in 15 mins

1 onion
2 tbsp butter
1 lb/450 g closed cup
  mushrooms
1 tsp tomato paste
1 tsp coarse grain mustard
⅔ cup sour cream
1 tsp paprika

salt and pepper
chopped fresh parsley,
  to garnish

1 Chop the onion finely. Heat the butter in a large, heavy-bottom skillet. Add the onion and cook gently for 5–10 minutes, until soft. Meanwhile, trim and quarter the mushrooms.

1

2 Add the mushrooms to the skillet and stir-fry for a few minutes until they start to soften. Stir in the tomato paste and mustard, then add the sour cream. Cook gently, stirring constantly, for 5 minutes.

3 Stir in the paprika and season to taste with salt and pepper. Garnish with chopped parsley and serve at once.

2

3

vegetable medley

$$$

- serves 4
- prepared in 15 mins
- cooks in 20 - 25 mins

1 large eggplant

2 zucchini

6 tbsp vegetable ghee or oil

1 large onion, quartered and sliced

2 garlic cloves, crushed

1-2 fresh green chilies, seeded and chopped, or 1-2 tsp minced chili

2 tsp ground coriander

2 tsp cumin seeds

1 tsp ground turmeric

1 tsp garam masala

14 oz/400 g can chopped tomatoes

½ pint/1¼ cups vegetable stock or water

salt and pepper

14 oz/400 g can garbanzo beans, drained and rinsed

2 tbsp chopped mint

¼ pint/⅔ cup heavy cream

1 Trim the leaf end off eggplant and cut into cubes. Trim and slice the zucchini.

2 Heat the ghee or oil in a saucepan and fry the eggplant, zucchini, onion, garlic and chillies over a low heat, stirring frequently, for about 5 minutes, adding a little more oil to the pan, if necessary.

1

3 Stir in the spices and cook for 30 seconds. Add the tomatoes and stock and season with salt and pepper to taste. Cook for 10 minutes.

4 Add the garbanzo beans to the pan and cook for a further 5 minutes.

3

5 Stir in the mint and cream and reheat gently. Taste and adjust the seasoning, if necessary. Transfer to a warm serving dish and serve hot with plain or pilau rice, or with parathas, if preferred.

5

spicy pasta

$$

- serves 4
- prepared in 10 mins
- cooks in 15 mins

9½ oz/275 g fresh pappardelle
3 tbsp peanut oil
2 garlic cloves, crushed
2 shallots, sliced
8 oz/225 g green beans, sliced
8 cherry tomatoes, halved
1 tsp chili flakes
4 tbsp crunchy peanut butter
⅔ cup coconut milk
1 tbsp tomato paste
sliced scallions, to garnish

1 Bring a large, heavy-bottom pan of lightly salted water to a boil. Add the pasta, return to a boil, and cook for 5–6 minutes.

2 Heat the peanut oil in a preheated wok or large skillet. Add the garlic and shallots, and stir-fry for 1 minute.

3 Drain the pasta thoroughly. Add the green beans and drained pasta to the wok, and stir-fry for 5 minutes. Add the cherry tomatoes to the wok and mix well.

4 Mix the chili flakes, peanut butter, coconut milk, and tomato paste together in a bowl.

5 Pour the chili mixture over the pasta, toss well to combine, and heat through. Transfer to warmed serving dishes and garnish with sliced scallions. Serve immediately.

3 3 5

chili with cheese pot pie

$$

- serves 4
- prepared in 25 mins
- cooks in 20 mins

1 tbsp corn oil
2 garlic cloves, crushed
1 red bell pepper, seeded and diced
1 green bell pepper, seeded and diced
1 celery stalk, diced
1 tsp hot chili powder
2 cups canned chopped tomatoes
1½ cups canned corn kernels, drained
1 cup canned kidney beans, drained and rinsed
2 tbsp chopped cilantro

salt and pepper
cilantro sprigs, to garnish
tomato and avocado salad, to serve

TOPPING
¾ cup cornmeal
1 tbsp all-purpose flour
½ tsp salt
2 tsp baking powder
1 egg, beaten
6 tbsp milk
1 tbsp corn oil
1 cup grated sharp Cheddar cheese

1 Heat the corn oil in a large skillet and gently cook the garlic and the diced bell peppers and celery for 5–6 minutes until just soft.

2 Stir in the chili powder, tomatoes, corn kernels, beans, and seasoning. Bring to a boil and simmer the mixture for 10 minutes. Stir in the cilantro and spoon into an ovenproof dish.

3 To make the topping, mix together the cornmeal, flour, salt, and baking powder. Make a well in the center, add the egg, milk, and oil and beat until a smooth batter is formed.

4 Spoon over the bell pepper and corn mixture and sprinkle with the grated cheese. Bake in a preheated oven, at 425°F/220°C, for 25–30 minutes, until golden and firm.

5 Garnish with the cilantro sprigs and serve the pie immediately with a tomato and avocado salad.

desserts

Just because you're short of time there is no excuse for

omitting dessert or serving boring old ice cream. From Caramel

Bananas to Quick Tiramisù, there are fabulous sweet treats with an

individual touch that will cost little in time or money.

Who could possibly resist?

caramel bananas

$$

- serves 4
- prepared in 10 mins
- cooks in 20 mins

4 ripe medium bananas

3 tbsp lemon juice

generous 1 cup superfine sugar

4 tbsp cold water

2 tbsp sesame seeds

⅔ cup lowfat plain yogurt

1 tbsp confectioners' sugar

1 tsp vanilla extract

shredded lemon rind and
shredded lime rind, to
decorate

1 Peel the bananas and cut into 2 inch/5 cm pieces. Place the banana pieces in a bowl, spoon over the lemon juice, and stir well to coat—this will help prevent the bananas from discoloring.

2 Place the sugar and water in a small pan and heat gently, stirring constantly, until the sugar dissolves. Bring to a boil and cook for 5–6 minutes until the mixture turns golden brown.

3 Meanwhile, drain the bananas and blot with paper towels to dry. Line a cookie sheet or board with baking parchment and arrange the bananas, well spaced apart, on top.

4 When the caramel is ready, drizzle it over the bananas, working quickly because the caramel sets almost instantly. Sprinkle the sesame seeds over the caramelized bananas and set aside to cool for 10 minutes.

5 Combine the yogurt, confectioners' sugar, and vanilla extract.

6 Peel the bananas away from the baking parchment and arrange on serving plates.

7 Serve the yogurt as a dip, decorated with the shredded lemon and lime rind.

1   3   4

$

sponge cake*

- serves 4
- prepared in 11 mins
- cooks in 9 mins

1¼ sticks butter or
  margarine
4 tbsp corn syrup
6 tbsp superfine sugar
2 eggs
1 cup self-rising flour

1 tsp baking powder
about 2 tbsp warm water
stirred custard, to serve

2

3

4

1 Grease a 2³/₄-pint/1.5-liter heatproof microwavable basin with a small amount of the butter. Spoon the corn syrup into the greased basin.

2 Cream the remaining butter with the sugar until light and fluffy. Gradually add the eggs, beating well after each addition.

3 Sift the flour and baking powder together, then fold into the creamed mixture using a large metal spoon. Add enough water to give a soft, dropping consistency. Spoon into the heatproof basin and smooth the surface.

4 Cover the basin with microwave-proof plastic wrap, leaving a small space to let air escape. Microwave on HIGH power for 4 minutes, then remove the sponge from the microwave oven and let stand for 5 minutes, while it continues to cook.

5 Turn the sponge out onto a warmed serving plate. Serve with custard.

* This recipe is cooked in a microwave

french toast

$

- serves 6
- prepared in 10 mins
- cooks in 15 mins

2 eggs
generous ⅓ cup milk
pinch of ground cinnamon
6 slices of white bread,
  crusts removed
4 oz/115 g unsalted butter

1 tbsp corn oil
generous ¼ cup brown
  sugar
4 tbsp golden syrup

1 Using a fork, beat the eggs with 6 tablespoons of the milk and the cinnamon in a large, shallow dish. Cut the bread into triangles and place in the dish, in batches if necessary, to soak for 2–3 minutes.

1

2 Melt half the butter with half the oil in a heavy-bottom skillet. Add the bread triangles, in batches, and cook for 2 minutes on each side, or until golden brown, adding a little more butter and oil as necessary. Remove with a spatula, drain on paper towels, transfer to serving plates, and keep warm.

2

3 Add the remaining butter and milk to the skillet with the sugar and golden syrup and cook, stirring constantly, until hot and bubbling. Pour the toffee sauce over the bread triangles and serve.

3

cinnamon baked pears

$$

- serves 4
- prepared in 10 mins
- cooks in 30 mins

4 ripe pears
2 tbsp lemon juice
¼ cup light brown sugar
1 tsp ground cinnamon
¼ cup lowfat spread
scant 2 cups lowfat custard
strips of lemon rind, to decorate

1 Preheat the oven to 400°F/ 200°C. Core and peel the pears, then slice in half lengthwise and brush all over with the lemon juice. Place the pears, cored-side down, in a small nonstick roasting pan.

2 Place the sugar, cinnamon, and lowfat spread in a small pan and heat gently, stirring constantly, until the sugar has melted. Keep the heat low to prevent too much water

evaporating from the lowfat spread. Spoon the mixture over the pears, then bake in the preheated oven, occasionally spooning the sugar mixture over the fruit, for 20–25 minutes, or until the fruit is tender and golden.

3 Heat the custard until piping hot and spoon over 4 warmed dessert plates. Arrange 2 pear halves on each plate, decorate with strips of lemon rind, and serve.

1   2   2

quick tiramisù

$$$

- serves 4
- prepared in 15 mins
- cooks in 0 mins

1 cup mascarpone or whole soft
  cheese
1 egg, separated
2 tbsp plain yogurt
2 tbsp superfine sugar

2 tbsp dark rum
2 tbsp strong black coffee
8 ladyfingers
2 tbsp grated semisweet
  chocolate

1   Place the cheese in a large bowl, then add the egg yolk and yogurt and, using a wooden spoon, beat until smooth.

2   Using a whisk, whisk the egg white in a separate spotlessly clean, greasefree bowl until stiff but not dry, then whisk in the sugar and carefully fold into the cheese mixture.

3   Spoon half of the mixture into 4 tall sundae glasses.

4   Mix the rum and coffee together in a shallow dish. Dip the ladyfingers briefly into the rum mixture, then break them in half or into smaller pieces, if necessary, and divide between the glasses.

5   Stir any of the remaining rum and coffee mixture into the remaining cheese and spoon over the top.

6   Sprinkle with grated chocolate and serve immediately. Alternatively, chill in the refrigerator until required.

pancake pieces

- serves 4
- prepared in 15 mins
- cooks in 10 mins

2 tbsp superfine sugar
1 tsp ground cinnamon
1 cup all-purpose flour
pinch of salt
2 eggs, lightly beaten
½ cup milk

14 oz/400 g canned apricot
 halves in syrup
corn oil, for brushing

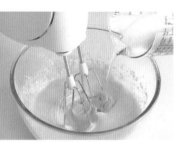

1 Place the sugar and cinnamon in a bowl and stir to mix, then reserve.

2 Sift the flour and salt into a separate bowl. Whisk the eggs and milk into the flour and continue whisking to make a smooth batter.

3 Drain the apricot halves, reserving the syrup, then whisk the syrup into the batter until combined. Coarsely chop the apricots and reserve.

4 Heat a large crêpe pan or heavy-bottom skillet and brush with oil. Pour in the batter and cook over medium heat for 4–5 minutes, or until the underside is golden brown. Turn over with a palette knife and cook the second side for 4 minutes, or until golden. Tear the pancake into bite-size pieces with 2 spoons or forks.

5 Add the apricots to the crêpe pan and heat through briefly. Divide the pancake pieces and apricots between 4 serving plates. Sprinkle with the sugar and cinnamon mixture and serve immediately.

apple fritters

$

- serves 4
- prepared in 10 mins
- cooks in 10 mins

corn oil, for deep-frying
1 large egg
pinch of salt
¾ cup water
scant ½ cup all-purpose flour
2 tsp ground cinnamon

4 tbsp superfine sugar
4 eating apples, peeled and
    cored

1 Pour the corn oil into a deep-fryer or large, heavy-bottom pan and heat to 350–375°F/180–190°C, or until a cube of bread browns in 30 seconds.

2 Meanwhile, using an electric mixer, beat the egg and salt together until frothy, then quickly whisk in the water and flour. Do not overbeat the batter—it doesn't matter if it isn't completely smooth.

3 Mix the cinnamon and sugar together in a shallow dish and reserve.

4 Slice the apples into ¼-inch/5-mm thick rings. Spear with a fork, 1 slice at a time, and dip in the batter to coat. Add to the hot oil, in batches, and cook for 1 minute on each side, or until golden and puffed up. Remove with a slotted spoon and drain on paper towels. Keep warm while you cook the remaining batches. Transfer to a large serving plate and sprinkle with the cinnamon sugar, then serve.

peach & apple cobbler

$$

- serves 4-6
- prepared in 15 mins
- cooks in 30 mins

1 cooking apple

2 eating apples

½ cup cold water

**14 oz/400 g canned peach slices
in fruit juice, drained**

scant ⅝ cup all-purpose flour

⅝ cup rolled oats

**generous ¼ cup firmly packed
raw brown sugar**

**2 oz/55 g polyunsaturated
spread**

**custard made with skim milk,
lowfat plain mascarpone
cheese, or yogurt, to serve**

1 Preheat the oven to 375°F/ 190°C. Peel, core, and slice the apples and put into a small pan with the water. Bring to a boil, then cover and let simmer, stirring occasionally, for 4–5 minutes, or until just tender. Remove from the heat and drain away any excess liquid. Stir the drained peach slices into the apple and transfer the fruit to a 4-cup ovenproof dish.

2 Meanwhile, combine the flour, oats, and sugar in a mixing bowl. Rub in the spread with your fingertips until the mixture resembles fine bread crumbs.

3 Sprinkle the cobbler topping evenly over the fruit and bake in the preheated oven for 20 minutes, or until golden brown. Serve warm with custard made with skim milk, or lowfat plain mascarpone cheese, or yogurt. This dessert is best eaten on the day it is made—any leftover cobbler should be stored in the refrigerator and consumed within 24 hours.

1   1   2

index

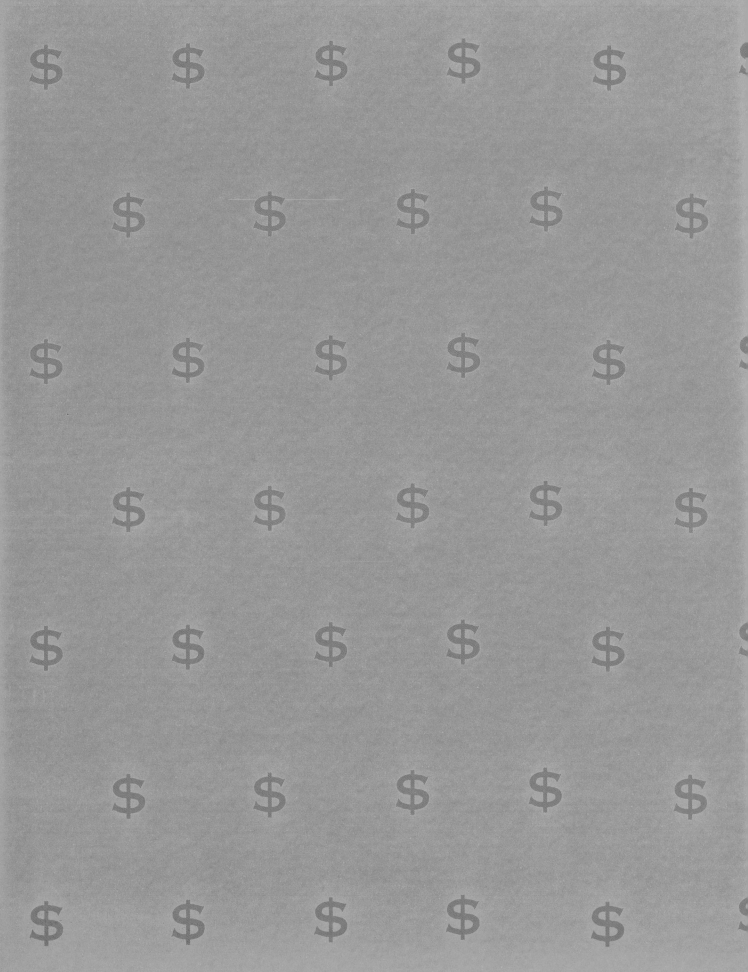